MW01199256

Dream Big
&
Have Fun!

Sarah Blossom
Ware

With heartfelt thanks to so many of my friends and family members for their encouragement, feedback and photos.

With special thanks to the Vickery family for allowing me to tell their stories along with my own.

Thank you to Andrea Shaw for the nudge: "You should write a coffee table book!"

I am the product of a hillbilly upbringing by hippie parents from Cleveland. These are some of my childhood memories.

In loving dedication to my wonderfully unique parents, George and Judy Kuharick. In loving memory of my wonderfully unique Granny, Ollie Vickery.

ISBN-13: 978-1494941222
ISBN-10: 1494941228

Cover design by Rachel Chojnacki

Hillbilly Justice on the School Bus

Table of Contents

Cowboy Boots

My parents were hippies. My parents are hippies. My middle name is Blossom. For my mother's 50th birthday she got a navel piercing. My father is now 63 years old and sports a ponytail. As a teenager I rebelled by becoming conservative.

I believe that everything in my life has been divinely ordered, despite the fact that most things in my life have seemed completely random. I ended up living in the Netherlands and receiving my doctorate degree because of a seemingly random blanket e-mail. And I grew up in the Ozark Foothills of Northwest Arkansas because of a seemingly random choice by my parents when I was three years old.

I was born in Cleveland, Ohio in 1974 and my brother George was born a little over a year later. We lived right in downtown Cleveland on East 33rd Street. We had running water and a phone and electricity and close access to grocery stores and all sorts of other amenities provided by a big city. This all changed in the spring of 1977.

My parents were avid hikers and campers. Their most recent excursion was in the mountains of Pennsylvania, and they were searching for their next vacation destination. It just so happened that my dad's brother, Uncle Rich, had a friend who traveled throughout the U.S. in an old ice cream truck. You may be wondering, as did I, whether his friend actually sold ice cream out of his truck to fund his travels. He did not. The ice cream truck had been demoted merely to an RV status. Well, the ice cream man told Uncle Rich about how much he enjoyed the Ozark Mountains of Arkansas. Based on the recommendation of the ice cream man, Northwest Arkansas became my parents' next vacation destination.

I still remember standing behind the glass door at my grandparents' house on East 66th Street waving good-bye as they left. George and I were the only grandchildren, and the time passed quickly because I loved spending time with Grandma and Grandpa.

When my parents returned, my happy eyes met theirs but then were quickly drawn downward. Feelings of amusement and confusion washed over me as I stared down at ...two new pairs of cowboy boots. Then, my parents excitedly dropped the bombshell - we were moving to Arkansas! A chaotic whirlwind of events followed. There were emotional pleas from family members to reconsider. Nearly all of our belongings were sold, and my parents purchased a green International Harvester Travelall, which was a sort of hippie SUV of its day. They loaded the Travelall with whatever belongings would fit, plus the four of us and my dog Bonzo. Within three weeks time, we left downtown Cleveland far behind.

The Back Forty

We pulled in to Fayetteville, Arkansas without a plan in the world for where we would stay. As we wound around Highway 71B, my parents spotted a quaint little hillside trailer park advertising places for rent. Dad stopped to inquire at the caretaker's house, which George and I later called The Man's House. My Dad can be quite the talker, and he was gone for some time, but when he came back he was wielding keys to our new (used) trailer rental. There is certainly no shortage of characters in this world, and it turned out that The Man at The Man's House was a cartoonist who specialized in Woody Woodpecker.

Fayetteville was nothing like Cleveland, except that it was also a city. George and I loved living by The Man's House. It was located very near a Baskin Robbins with its thirty-one scrumptious flavors of ice cream. It was also near Wilson Park, which had two playgrounds and a swimming pool. I guess these conveniences were too much for Mom and Dad, because we only stayed by The Man's House for about a month. Then my Dad came home one day and announced that he had just bought the most perfect tract of land.

We moved onto forty acres of wooded land on top of Hoot Owl Mountain – literally the Back Forty. Never mind that there was no electricity there. Or plumbing. Or house. No problem! We lived in a huge army tent for several months while my parents built a cabin with the help of our "neighbors" the Emersons who lived several miles away. Mr. Emerson taught Dad how to use a chainsaw to cut down trees. Since there was no electricity, the entire cabin was built using chainsaws, hand saws, hammers and nails. After the log frame was assembled, Dad nailed solid sheets of wood paneling all around the four sides of the house. Then he drew a rectangle and some squares and used his chainsaw to cut out holes to create the door and some windows. The imagery that comes to my mind is that this is exactly the way that Bugs Bunny and Wile E. Coyote would build their cabins.

No, this was not a White Oak Lodge cabin. This was a Back Forty cabin, but it was fancy because it had two stories. The bottom story was one large open room that served as the kitchen/dining room/living room and the top story was a large open sleeping loft. My brother Henry was born during the cabin years, and his crib was a dresser drawer that was set on the floor in the loft. The carpet on the ground floor was actually artificial turf – the green plastic stuff. It was quite a step up from the tent. I did not mention where the bathroom was in the cabin. That's because there wasn't one.

But there was a front porch. On summer nights, I would read books by Coleman lantern light. When I was about six years old, my grandparents gave me the wonderful gift of the entire Little House on the Prairie book series. I loved reading about the adventures of young Laura Ingalls. I didn't realize until many years later that I wasn't supposed to be able to relate to her life so well.

And so I found myself ultimately plucked out of Cleveland, one of the most populated cities in the U.S., and set down in the middle of nowhere. My youth was lived out in Cove Creek

Community, just south of Hogeye and northeast of Bug Scuffle, not far from Devil's Den.

Dad

My dad fully embraced the Southern lifestyle from day one. He took on the slow, Southern drawl both in speech and life in general. Dad really didn't get worked up about anything. Once when I was 15 years old, I came home around 3 am after running around with Jonathan. Jonathan is now my husband, but then he was a 17-year-old boy who had kept me out way too late. My mother had waited up and understandably laid into me in a bit of a panic: "Where *were* you?! Do you have any idea what time it is?! What could you have *possibly* been thinking coming home so late?! What type of punishment do you think you deserve for this?!" My dad walked into the living room, and Mom commenced to frantically telling him what I had done and finally said, "George, you talk to her!" Dad looked me straight in the eyes and calmly stated, "3 o'clock is not a time to be coming home. It's a time to be going fishing." And he picked up his pole and walked out the door.

Dad loved to fish. He truly enjoyed the experience of fishing for hours on end, regardless of whether or not he was catching them. Some weekends when Dad was on duty, he would lead George and me traipsing across the mountaintop to fish in an unknown pond. There were no roads or even trails, so I was always amazed that we could make it there and back home. These were wonderful adventures in the wilderness. Dad would point out trees and teach us the names: oak, elm, maple and dogwood. The dogwoods are a stunning display of white in the Ozarks in the spring. As much as I have fond memories of our fishing trips with Dad, I also remember being completely parched because the only refreshments he would bring were alcoholic, and he wouldn't share.

On one occasion, Dad took the boys on an excursion to Eck Lake. All three of them left with shoes on, but the boys returned bare-footed. Mom began the interrogation: "George, what happened to their shoes?" Dad: "I don't know." "George and Henry, where are your shoes?" "We don't know," they replied with innocent eyes. Try as she might, my mom was not able to crack this case. It was only a couple of years ago that Dad finally told her what had happened. Eck Lake had been drained, and the boys couldn't resist a super big mud hole. They ran into it to play, but they immediately started sinking like it was quick sand. My dad struggled to free them, but their shoes were sacrificed in the process. I guess I can understand why Dad would be afraid to tell Mom that the kids were almost sucked into the bottom of Eck Lake.

Dad was always reading. I seldom remember him without a thick paperback novel somehow stuffed into a back pocket of his Rustler jeans, just to the right of his plumber's crack. He would read newspapers and comic books and historical documentaries and science fictional thrillers. He would even read encyclopedias from cover to cover (who does that?). In the years after we got electricity, Dad would always require us to watch Jeopardy at 4 pm if school was canceled due to weather. He said it was so that we would get some schooling for the day, but I think he just wanted to show off because he always smoked all of the categories.

We told him *he* should be a contestant on Jeopardy since he was full of useless trivia. If anyone knows how to hook him up, then contact me.

Dad also enjoyed playing cards and board games, but Mom did not. Dad taught me at a very young age how to play Monopoly and Pinochle and all sorts of other fun games that were really way beyond my years. I remember that he was patient with me but did not show much mercy. Perhaps that is why I am so competitive now. Dad and I had a you-snooze-you-lose rule when playing Monopoly such that when a person landed on the opponent's property, no rent was owed unless that opponent caught it and asked for payment. During the rare times that Mom would play, the guilty party (Dad or I) would wait until the next person's turn and then point out snickering to Mom that she'd missed collecting rent (and she *always* missed collecting rent). She would get so angry and call us cheaters, but it's not cheating if that's your rule.

Mom

My mom embraced the Southern lifestyle in so far as she had to in order to survive. To this day, Mom speaks exactly the same way as she did living and growing up in downtown Cleveland – very fast and with a distinctly Midwest accent. Even though she was less enamored than Dad with the hillbilly lifestyle, my mother from Cleveland did learn how to be a darn good mountain woman. Mrs. Emerson taught her a lot of what she learned, including how to cook brown beans and cornbread and how to can pickles. Mrs. Emerson also taught Mom how to milk a goat and how to pee and poop in the woods. Other things Mom taught herself out of necessity. She figured out how to cook Boston brown bread in a metal coffee can over a campfire, and she learned how to make homemade yogurt from an article in the Mother Earth News. Mom also learned how to shoot snakes with a shotgun, which was a necessity since it was quite common to run across poisonous rattlesnakes, copperheads and cottonmouths.

Even everyday household chores like doing the laundry were made insurmountably difficult without running water and electricity. Dad worked six to seven days per week at Campbell's Soup, so that left the insurmountable household chores to Mom. Every Saturday was laundry day – all day. Mom would gather up seven days' worth of dirty clothes for six people into big black trash bags and load these into the car. Us kids would fit in between and on top of the bags wherever there was room, and we'd take a twenty-minute trip in to Prairie Grove to the laundry mat.

George and I always found it very exciting to load the quarters into their slots on the washing machines and shove the slots forward to start the wash cycles. After this task was accomplished, the excitement was over and the waiting began. There was a bit of a pick-me-up when it was time to transfer the clothes to the dryers, and then more waiting. If the weather was nice enough, we would save money on dryers and bring the wet clothes back home to dry on the clothesline. Hours and hours of waiting. Sometimes we would walk to the library and bring books back to read. Most of the time, we were just really bored.

Mom always did the best she could with what we had, which was nothing. I know that now, but I didn't know it then, so she did a good job. What do kids remember fondly when there are no materialistic items present? One memory that stands out from my childhood is when Mom helped George and me make homemade Christmas ornaments in the loft of the cabin when I was four or five years old. Mom hand-drew pictures of angels, stars and Christmas trees on some stiff yellowed paper. We colored the pictures with crayons and then cut out the ornaments. Mom stabbed a ragged hole at the top of each ornament with the tip of a knife and we looped yarn through and tied them off. I can still clearly picture black lines on the back of the ornaments. Now

I know that the stiff paper that we used must have been some type of free scrap paper that Mom picked up from somewhere. The ornaments were so beautiful hanging on the branches of our little Charlie Brown Christmas tree.

I also remember that Mom was an interesting driver. She didn't get her driver's license until she and Dad moved to Arkansas. She claims that she never needed one until then, but I have an inkling that maybe no officer would pass her in Cleveland. Mom always drove one speed, around 40 mph, whether she was on dirt road or blacktop. This was a flying speed when on the dirt roads and a crawling turtle's pace when on the blacktop. One day, a friend of mine from high school confided in me under his breath that he was driving behind my mom on his way home from school and that she was drunk. He mimicked how she was leaning forward and grasping the steering wheel tightly as she crawled along at about 40 mph. Such a silly boy. I told him that I had no doubt that he had observed all of this but that my mom didn't drink.

The Wishing Well

We had a well and a pond on our property. The well was about forty yards from the cabin and the pond was also about forty yards away but in the opposite direction. The well water was for drinking and cooking, and the pond water was for bathing and general cleaning.

A lot of time and physical labor went into preparation for a bath. My mother would haul five-gallon buckets of water up from the pond. She would pour some of the water directly into the bath tub, which was a hard plastic kiddie pool, and she would heat some of the water in a large pot on the propane stove. She would pour the hot water into the bathtub so that it wasn't too cold when we got in to bathe. The bath water was brownish-green: brown from disturbing the water when scooping it into the bucket and green from algae and frog eggs. I *guess* we were cleaner when we came out than when we went in. Or maybe Mom was just carrying out the motions because mothers were supposed to bathe their children.

I remember that my mom was always hauling water. If it wasn't from the pond, it was from the well. Our well looked just like the stereotypical wishing well from fairy tales. There was a circular wall of rocks built up around it so that you couldn't accidentally fall in. And it had the bucket attached to the rope and the hand crank. Mom used to pour water from the bucket into empty milk jugs and carry those to the house.

All of this physical labor was hard on my mother, and it was hard on her wedding ring. One day the setting on her ring became loose and her half-carat diamond fell into the well while she was fetching water. A search and recovery team was formed with some of the neighbors. Dad was hoisted into the well with the rope. He made it to the bottom of the well and shone his flashlight around trying to locate the diamond. After a few minutes of searching, Dad began to feel dizzy and had to be hoisted back out due to bad air in the well. I sometimes wonder if Mom didn't sacrifice her diamond in an act of desperation: "I wish I could go to the ball!" – chunk! Sorry, Mom, your wish didn't come true.

I'm not one to start legends, but for all you treasure seekers out there, that half-carat diamond still rests at the bottom of that wishing well.

The Hot Seat

Our high-falootin' lifestyle was obviously attractive. Its grandiosity even managed to lure another family member away from downtown Cleveland to join in the fun. My mom's brother, Uncle Danny, drove down with whatever fit in his car when I was four years old. Then his car promptly died, but that was alright because it became his home at the curve in our driveway, just before the road took a steep turn downward. It was great fun having family close by.

After awhile, Uncle Danny decided to move out of his car and into the woods. He did not have a large army tent like us, though. It was more like a tarp draped over a fallen log. Even to a child, it seemed a little cramped. Uncle Danny lived on our property out of his car and in the woods for about a year.

During the summer of 1978, while Uncle Danny still lived near us, my family hosted its first and only big hillbilly party. I remember a keg and lots of people having fun. The main roads of our mountain were not well-maintained, so you can imagine what our driveway was like. It was about a quarter mile long and was more like a winding ravine than a road.

Our family car at this time was a 1965 Volkswagen Beetle, but today it was the party shuttle. Every half hour or so, my dad would take the Beetle down the ravine and pick up any guests who had gathered. I liked going on these shuttle missions because I liked the surprise of who might be waiting at the bottom.

On the third shuttle trip, I was sitting in the back seat with our guests when it got very warm. I told my dad, "It's really hot back here," to which he replied "It's an Arkansas summer." As we continued to drive, our guests also mentioned that it *was* really hot. As soon as we got to the cabin, we all jumped out. Dad touched the back seat, got a surprised look on his face, and then quickly flipped the back bench seat over. Flames jumped high into the air. The engine had caught fire. No one seemed particularly alarmed. The burning Beetle served as a great hillbilly bonfire for the party.

Summer Sausage

We were not self-sustaining by any means, but we did have goats that gave milk and chickens that laid eggs (although it was difficult to find them since the chickens were free-range and continually came up with new hiding places). Dad worked at Campbell's Soup Co. as a tool-and-dye maker. As an employee, he had access to the company store where he received discounted rates on scratch-and-dent cans and new t.v. dinner combinations that were being trialed. I remember eating a lot of Campbell's soup and t.v. dinners marked 'x-pack' and big bags of cheese butts (the crinkly ends from deli cheese - not to be confused with butt cheese, which the Urban Dictionary defines as lint from your butt). And a lot of hot dogs, but I think those were from the regular store. So you see, even though we were poor, we ate rich.

But back to the animals, the goats. Some people say that goat milk is an acquired taste. It's not. It's just disgusting. If it were an acquired taste, I would have acquired it. And I didn't. Even so, I really, really, really wanted to milk a goat. My goat's name was Summer. Summer was a wonderful white goat, and my mom promised that I would be able to milk her when I turned eight years old the following year. But it wasn't meant to be.

Unlike the feral chickens, Summer and Billy the billy goat were enclosed in a pen surrounded by an electrified barbed wire fence. But this is no match for a goat. Summer and Billy escaped on a regular basis and had to be herded back into the pen.

We were able to move up the social ladder very quickly. By this time, we had moved on from the cabin and into every Arkansan's dream home, a two-bedroom trailer. We even got electricity and a phone *and* a bathroom, but there was still no running water. My sister Mary Jane was born during the trailer years.

One day when we came home, the trailer door was open. This by itself wasn't unusual since the trailer door didn't shut properly and often flung open. The unusual thing was that we found Billy inside munching on Dad's J.R.R. Tolkien series and Summer inside jumping on Mom and Dad's bed.

Mom and Dad shewed the goats out of the trailer. Mom, completely fed up with goats, yelled to Dad: "George, shoot those goats!" My father pulled out his shotgun and extinguished all of my dreams of goat milking right before my eyes. In case you're wondering, yes, this was a defining moment in my childhood. As if this wasn't enough for a seven-year-old girl, the entire mountainside came over the next day for a good old fashioned goat roast. *And* over the next several days, my dog Bonzo kept showing up with white tufts of fur in her mouth, all proud and mocking-like. My kind and sensitive husband has coined this my Summer Sausage story.

Public Parks and Drive-Ins

Most of our recreational activities were outdoors and nearly all of our recreational activities were free. The Arkansas summers were hot and sunny, and there were many ways to enjoy them, including parks, drive-in theaters and swimming holes.

My three favorite parks growing up were Wilson Park in Fayetteville, Devil's Den State Park in West Fork and the Prairie Grove Battlefield State Park in Prairie Grove.

Wilson Park, near The Man's House, is the first park I remember as a child. The coolest thing about Wilson Park was the addition of a magical fairy tale Lord-of-the-Rings type of castle in the early '80s designed specifically for kids to climb all over. The castle was built over a spring that flowed into a coy pond area, which then flowed into Scull Creek. There was a wonderful troll foot bridge that crossed over the flowing spring water. A black gate door with a huge lock guarded the opening of the spring, but it was easy to imagine as a child that behind this locked gate was a dungeon area where a princess was being held prisoner. The castle, which turned 30 years old in 2010, is still as magical now as it was then.

Devil's Den State Park was every bit as interesting as its name might suggest and much more beautiful. The Battlefield Park and Wilson Park were day trips, but we often camped overnight at Devil's Den. We would have sandwiches in the picnic areas and cook hot dogs over the camp fire. There were amazing trails with caves to explore and wet-weather waterfalls to walk through. It was always a lot of fun to participate in the sack race, watermelon spitting contest and cow chip toss at the Annual Devil's Den Games held every 4th of July.

The Prairie Grove Battlefield State Park was established in 1908 to commemorate the site where the Battle of Prairie Grove was fought during the Civil War. The best part about the Battlefield Park was the presence of two massive tank-like M40 self-propelled artillery vehicles parked next to the playground. George and I would climb all around on top of them and out onto the ends of the barrels of the canons. The best, best part about the tanks, as we called them, is that we could crawl underneath them and pop up through the hatches and into the control areas where we could jockey the levers around and push buttons.

The tanks were removed sometime in the '80s because some people complained that they post-dated the Civil War. Despite their historical inaccuracy, I was so sad to see them go. As I look back now, I suppose it was a rather macabre form of entertainment, as these tanks almost certainly were involved in the deaths of soldiers and/or civilians during their stints in WW II. Nevertheless, a fond childhood memory is eternally etched as a fond childhood memory.

A couple of times each summer we would load up and go to see a drive-in movie. There were actually two drive-in theaters in Fayetteville when I was growing up: the 112 Drive-In and the 62 Drive-In, both named for the highways they were on. The 112 Drive-In was in north Fayetteville, which was further away, so we usually went to the 62 Drive-In, which was my favorite. Every showing was a double feature. The early movie was for kids and the late movie was for adults. We would usually stay for both, but I never really understood what was going on in the second movie and had to cover my eyes a lot.

Getting in to the 62 Drive-In was always a covert mission because there was a charge per person instead of per car load. As we would near the entrance gate, Dad would instruct George and me to curl up in the floorboards and Mom would cover us up with blankets. We somehow knew that this was our only shot at admission (probably because we were told that), so we were always very still and quiet. Worked every time! Once we were parked, we would spring up from the floorboards and sprint to the playground area just below the big screen and play until the movie started showing.

I remember watching one of the Herbie the Love Bug movies, The Shaggy D.A., Swamp Thing (tackiest movie ever, besides Love Bug and Shaggy D.A.), and many showings of Star Wars. Watching the alien bar scene in the original Star Wars on the big screen was the absolute best! A Wal-Mart Supercenter is now on the site of the old 62 Drive-In, but the 112 Drive-In still shows movies every summer. Admission is $7 per adult and $3 for children ages 6-12.

What Happens at the Blue Hole
Stays at the Blue Hole

Another summertime family favorite was going swimming in the Blue Hole. The Blue Hole was a long way down a dirt road. There was one spot in the road that always had standing water across it. We never knew how deep the water was, because the depth was constantly changing depending on the amount of rainfall we'd received and whether the road had gotten washed out or not since the last crossing. Sometimes Dad would stop the car and get out and survey the situation from several angles, much like a golfer trying to read the lay of the green before an important putt. In the end, Dad's approach would always be the same. He would back up the car and get a running start at it and just plow right through the middle. Sometimes we sped on through to the other side without much incidence. Sometimes the water would cover the entire hood and the force of our quick approach would gently float us across. The latter generally resulted in a stall-out. We would just wait awhile until the car dried out, then start it back up and get on our way.

The Blue Hole *was* blue, but it would have more aptly been named the Snake Hole. If no other swimmers were present when we arrived, we had to take a few minutes to throw rocks in to scare the snakes away before entering the water. On the other hand, if it was too crowded when we arrived, we would yell "snake!" to clear people out. The Blue Hole was an unusually deep, wide pool of water in an otherwise very narrow and shallow creek. There was a large rock bluff on the far side of the deep pool. We could access the bluff by swimming to a rock ledge and then hoisting ourselves out of the water. We would then climb to the top of the bluff and jump off. It was really a beautiful swimming hole.

George and I learned to swim in the Blue Hole. Dad said, "Are you ready to learn how to swim?" I said yes, and he threw me out into the deep water and let my survival instinct kick in. I'm such a sucker paying for swimming lessons for my daughters through the park district.

One day my dad went swimming in the Blue Hole with his good friend - we'll call him Leroy, and Leroy's wife, two kids and mother-in-law. Dad and Leroy had been drinking quite heavily, as they were prone to do, when a car load of people they didn't know pulled up and began swimming. After a few minutes, one of the newcomers got out of the water, walked over to his towel, and flung it up into the air with a very deliberate motion. He then began ranting and raving and gave a general address to the swimmers: "Where's my watch?! I had it here and now it's gone! I want to know which one of y'all stole my watch!" No one fessed up, and he turned his attention to Leroy specifically. "Where's my watch???"

Without saying a word, Leroy got out of the Blue Hole, walked over to his truck, and walked back with his deer rifle. He stared at his accuser and carefully addressed him: "I don't know where *you're* from, but where *I'm* from we don't take kindly to being accused of thievery." Leroy then instructed everyone to line up in a straight line and said, "I want everyone to strip down completely naked. And if I don't find that watch on anyone, I'm going to shoot *you!*" – he pointed his rifle at the stranger. My dad knew that Leroy was half crazy, but he was stifling the urge to laugh while standing rigidly in line at gun point. It was very quiet until Leroy's mother-in-law defiantly broke the silence by declaring, "You're gonna have to shoot me first before I git naked in front of you and all these people here!"

The accusing stranger surveyed the situation and came to the realization that he was out-crazied. He began backtracking: "Oh, I was mistaken. I must've left my watch in my truck or something. Heck, I don't even own a watch." Then he and his friends took off running towards his truck and sped away. Since no one actually got naked or shot, Dad and Leroy and the gang were basically unfazed by the encounter and continued with their swim.

When Leroy finally arrived back home, he found two Prairie Grove police officers waiting in his driveway. "We heard you pulled a pistol on some people at the Blue hole. They got your license plate number and called it in." Leroy responded truthfully, "You can search my house. I don't even own a pistol." The officers just shrugged at one another and decided not to pursue the report any further.

All of Our Cars Were Brown and Old

We had *so* many vehicles growing up. I'm sure you can guess by now that it wasn't because we were wealthy. It was because all these crappy old vehicles were always breaking down. Until I was around nine years old, our cars were of various colors, usually green or white, but later Mom and Dad developed an unwavering loyalty to the color brown. And regardless of the color, they were always old.

Mom and Dad and George and I moved to Arkansas in the Green Truck (as George and I called it) with whatever worldly possessions fit with us. The Green Truck was a 1965 International Harvester Travelall, which was an old school SUV. The Green Truck was green, and it became someone's house when Dad sold it.

Of course, we also had the 1965 Volkswagen Bonfire, I mean Beetle. It was white/charcoal. For a brief time, we had a totally pimped out forest green Cadillac with power door locks and windows and adjustable seats and food trays in the back. Someone that Dad worked with at Campbell's Soup used to live in this Cadillac in the Campbell's Soup parking lot. The guy eventually got an apartment and sold his house to Dad. Before long, the power seat on the driver's side got stuck in the low position where Dad would set it. Mom had to sit on three pillows just to see out of the windshield.

Then there was the 1962 red, white and primer colored International Harvester Scout. It was a 4-wheel drive recreational vehicle made to compete with the Jeep. It was great for the dirt road mountain, but it was never really meant for highway driving. We drove it to Ohio and back one year visiting relatives.

Dad didn't seem to mind driving all of these cars, but they were nearly the end of Mom. One day Mom went to start the Scout after she got out of nursing classes at the University of Arkansas and the carburetor caught on fire. This was the proverbial straw that broke the camel's back. Mom walked to Jose's Mexican Restaurant and Cantina on Dickson Street, plopped down on a bar stool, ordered a shot and a beer, and bummed a cigarette (she didn't smoke). She called Dad from the restaurant phone and told him that he had to come and pick her up because she was having a nervous breakdown. The Scout was towed to the bottom of our driveway where it sat for a couple of years. One day, Mr. Emerson asked Dad if he'd sold the Scout because he'd seen it hitched up to the back of a tow truck heading in to Fayetteville. Dad hadn't sold it, and we never found out what happened to it. Someone almost certainly sold it to a salvage yard and probably got a couple hundred dollars out of it for scrap metal.

Flash forward to the brown car years. We had a huge brown Chevy pick-up truck with a 4-speed transmission plus a granny gear. Probably another one that should have never left the dirt roads but did. It had no power steering, and Mom had to rise up and stand on the clutch with both feet to shift it while driving.

We also had a brown Plymouth Fury, which Mom deemed the ugliest car she'd ever seen in her life - quite an award considering all of the other cars we'd owned. The vinyl top was all cracked and peeling on the outside of the car, and the fabric on the ceiling of the interior was all shredded. It dangled down like brown poop-colored Christmas tinsel, and we were continually wiping it out of our faces and ripping pieces off. Sadly for Mom, the Fury was not only the ugliest car we ever had but also the best running car we ever had. It just would not die. Mom finally declared that she was going to set a fire beneath it to end her misery, so Dad gave it away.

At one point, both of our (running) family vehicles were brown station wagons. When we were getting ready to go somewhere, all of us kids would always place bets: Are we going to take the brown station wagon *with* wood paneling or the brown station wagon *without* wood paneling? We weren't rooting for either one in particular.

More Car Stories

All of our old crappy cars were continually breaking down. We could not usually afford to pay someone to fix them, so Dad did most of that. He did not have any formal training as an auto mechanic, but this was one of the skills he picked up out of necessity. Sometimes the problem was an easy fix and sometimes it wasn't. I remember lots of clutches going out. If the parts were too expensive or too complicated to replace, it was time for a "new" vehicle.

Flat tires were a very frequent occurrence. The Kuharick family record for flat tires in one day stands at three. Fix-A-Flat was a staple. There were usually several cans rolling around in the trunk of each vehicle at any given time. My parents always bought used tires that were pre-balded but not yet flat, which means that these were the tires that other people felt were too dangerous to drive on the road and got rid of. I actually never witnessed the purchase of a set of brand new tires until after I got married. It seemed like such splurging.

I remember one time we were ready to go somewhere when George was about 10 years old. We conducted our usual walk around the car to check for flats, and this mission turned up positive. Dad wasn't home, so Mom asked George to change the flat, and he did. We got about halfway to Prairie Grove and were driving at a pretty good clip (nearly 40 mph) on the blacktop when all of the sudden we heard a horrible noise like amplified fingernails grinding on a chalkboard. We saw sparks shooting out of the back of the car and saw our "new" tire bounce over the fence and bound across the cow pasture and out of sight.

On another occasion when Mom was at work at the Washington County Health Department, all of the staff members were startled by a loud "boom!" When the nurses ran outside to see what had happened, they found that all of the windows of Mom's brown station wagon were shattered out. It was a bit terrifying. Who would have done such a thing, and in broad daylight? It turned out that the spare tire in the back of the car had gotten too hot in the Arkansas summer and exploded. My mother drove the car this way to pick up my brother Henry from his baseball game before driving home. What are you going to do???

It was my Senior year in high school when the brown car years finally subsided. My parents bought me my first car, a 1978 Dodge Aspen. It was white, and it was 1991. After I drove it for a couple of months, one of the headlights went out. A couple of weeks later I was driving home from Fayetteville after a late shift at KFC when the other headlight went out. I drove home the remaining ten miles in the dark using my blinking yellow hazard lights.

Granny

From the ages of three to five years old, my world consisted primarily of my parents, my brother George, an occasional "neighbor," goats, chickens, my Whippet dog Bonzo, mud puddles and wood piles. When I was five years old, my world became much bigger when I was introduced to Granny, my new babysitter, and Granny's vast extended family along with her. Granny lived on the adjacent mountain to ours, Blue Mountain a.k.a. Kelly Mountain, just across the blacktop. Granny was related to everyone, whether by blood or otherwise. She was greeted as Granny, Mom, or Aunt Ollie by everyone who walked through her door.

I have never known so many people in one family to have names starting with the letter "O". Granny was Ollie. She had a brother named Onnie, a son named Olan, and a daughter named Oma. Granny had seven children in all, from oldest to youngest: C.L., Lillian, Oma, LV, Norma (pronounced Normie), Rue and Olan. As a child, I had the most interactions with Olan, L.V. and Rue. Oma lived in Oklahoma, but everyone else lived within close proximity. Norma and L.V. lived on the far side of Kelly Mountain. Rue lived with Granny, and Olan lived just up the hill about 100 yards above her. Olan had four children: Cristal, Lisa, Corey and Josh. Corey was my age and Josh was George's age, so that was perfect for playing. And so the lives of the Kuharicks and the Vickerys were intermingled.

Although Granny's heritage is undocumented, Granny claimed to be one-quarter Black Dutch, which in this case is a Cherokee descent. Regardless of the lack of documentation, Granny looked 100% like an old Indian princess. She had long blackish-gray hair that flowed down to her calves, but the only time we saw its length was when she briefly unpinned it to re-wrap her bun. Granny always wore a modest short-sleeved one-piece dress that reached down to her ankles. Granny Vickery was very much like Granny Clampett from the Beverly Hillbillies in stature, spunk and shrilling voice.

Granny lived her entire life as we knew it within the confines of her humble home, namely sitting in her rocking chair in the living room. When we weren't playing outside, we were watching t.v. Every day at noon, Granny would announce, "You kids quit your scufflin'! My stories are fixin' to come on." Granny's stories were her daytime soaps. They would start with All My Children, then One Life to Live and then General Hospital. My favorite characters were Erica Kane, Tad Martin, and Luke and Laura Spencer, respectively.

Granny always put full effort into everything she set out to do. Colossians 3:23, "And whatsoever ye do, do it heartily, as to the Lord, and not unto men." Long before we met Granny, she had worked for 33 years peeling tomatoes for 3 cents a 14-quart bucket at the Kelly Canning Company. Granny often referred fondly to the 'canon' company. At a reunion of employees in 1985, Granny was presented with an award for #1 Woman Worker. I'm sure she was. I never saw her peel tomatoes, but I did see her pick blueberries. Some fun summer days, someone would arrive at Granny's house and load us up in the bed of a pick-up truck and take us in to Farmington, about 20 minutes away, to pick blueberries. It is not as easy as it sounds. It would take me about half an hour to fill one bucket, and the contents had much to be desired with stems and green berries. Granny was super fast at filling those buckets, and her berries were beautiful. She had a special technique using her thumbs to roll the berries off of the plants and into the buckets without any of the stems.

Granny was also exceptionally good at quilting. Granny had an electric sewing machine, and she was just as handy with that as she was at peeling tomatoes and picking blueberries. She would transform piles of old clothing and other materials into beautiful quilted masterpieces. Some of the quilts had very intricate designs. My favorite design was the basket pattern, but I also liked her star pattern a lot.

Granny had a tacking frame that hung from the ceiling of her living room. This was a rectangular shape made out of four sets of two small boards. When Granny needed to tack out a quilt, she would unwind the twine at the corners of the frame to lower it from the ceiling until it came down to about waist high. Then she would secure a sewn quilt onto the frame by sandwiching the edges in between the two sets of boards. Granny let us help her tack out the quilts. We would stand underneath the frame and loop short pieces of yarn through the center of the quilt squares with a large needle and then tie them off with simple knots.

Banging on the Barrel

Granny had a black rotary phone that was mounted on her wall near the front door, but Olan did not have phone service. Granny and Olan communicated by banging on 55-gallon steel drums. Granny would go out with her hammer to bang on the barrel. Bang, bang, bang. Olan would walk out his front door and yell, "Whoop! Mom!" Then they would yell back and forth whatever needed to be communicated.

Granny's phone almost never rang, unless there was a lightning strike nearby. This would cause the bell on the phone to make a very sluggish, half-hearted attempt at a ring. One afternoon, there was a lightning strike so close and powerful that it blew that black phone off of the wall and sent it sailing across the room.

The speaking that I had heard up until this time had been done by my parents, who came from Cleveland. The speaking that I heard at Granny's house was sometimes foreign and confusing to me. Dinner was lunch and supper was dinner. It's pert near time for dinner meant it was almost time for lunch (pretty near time). Pert near was not to be confused with ros'near, which was a piece of corn on the cob (roasting ear).

Granny and I went round and round one afternoon trying to communicate with one another. She kept saying to me: "Go git me a pin." I was wandering around all over the living room searching for a safety pin or a straight pin or a push pin or a clothes pin. The whole time, Granny kept saying, "A pin, a pin. Don't you know what a pin is?" Yes, I did, but I wasn't finding one. Finally, she got up reluctantly from her rocking chair and went to the kitchen and brought back a pen.

Despite Granny's best efforts to educate me in the hillbilly language, I was still lagging behind. In kindergarten one day, Mrs. Clark instructed us to use crayons to color a picture on some construction paper. She then told us to wad up our paper as part of the project. In my mind I was running the word wad over and over trying to make a connection. I thought I had figured it out and walked over to the sink in the classroom and ran water over my picture. Wad, wadder, water. I was very embarrassed when I saw the other kids crumpling their papers instead of wetting them. Needless to say, I ruined my art project.

I always felt like an outsider looking in, but make no mistake about it – I was definitely in the thick of it, a real Arkansas hillbilly.

Getting Churched

The Ozarks are smack dab in the middle of the Bible Belt of the South, where religion is not optional but required. There was never a question of *if* you went to church but *where* you went to church. George and I were both christened as babies at St. Vitus Catholic Church in Cleveland, but there were no Catholic churches anywhere near our Baptist mountain in Arkansas.

Our neighbors, the Emersons, were members of Little Elm Missionary Baptist Church in Farmington, which was about half an hour's drive away towards Fayetteville. Mrs. Emerson invited us to go to church incessantly as part of her Christian duty. My parents finally caved in and we eventually began attending fairly regularly. We were churched three times a week; twice on Sundays and once on Wednesday nights. Sundays were completely consumed with church. We went Sunday mornings from 10 am to noon, then went home and ate lunch, then napped, and then returned to church for the Sunday evening service. Wednesday evening services were necessary to jog people back to the truth after backsliding halfway through the week.

Most of the members at Little Elm were wealthy, at least relatively speaking. Many of them farmed cattle or chickens. We sang Southern Gospel songs from pew hymnals, and there was a choir led by John Robert Hart. What a voice! Some Sundays were especially exciting when one member or a group of members from the congregation would be highlighted by being announced and coming up to sing a prepared "special." My favorite specials were when John Robert would play the piano and sing with his son Wesley (who was my age) and his daughter Julie. Both John Robert and Wes are still quite sought-after musicians in Prairie Grove, Fayetteville and the surrounding area.

My sister Mary Jane was born three years after Henry and went under Granny's care after the standard six weeks. I mention this in the religion chapter because in Granny's eyes, Mary Jane was the Chosen One. Her birth was akin to the birth of the Baby Jesus Himself, and she could sin not. In the eyes of George and me, she was Joseph, and we plotted ways to throw her into the pit. We once falsely accused Mary Jane of swearing on the school bus and convinced my mother to wash her mouth out with soap. But we weren't *always* malicious, at least not consciously.

One Sunday, my mother's face flushed red when several members of the Little Elm congregation pointed out to her in whispered voices that Mary Jane, probably three years old at the time, was not sitting in a ladylike fashion and that she also did not have any underpants on. Somehow I got blamed for that because I had been charged with getting her dressed that morning. I thought I did a pretty decent job for a 10-year-old by managing to get her in a dress – just forgot one minor detail. Another Sunday, we got halfway home before Mom realized that Mary Jane wasn't in the car with us. When we drove back up to the church, we were confronted with a bunch of parishioners standing outside the front doors with confused looks on their faces and Mary Jane standing in the midst. Mom was embarrassed again and we got blamed again.

Old Time Religion

Smoking is apparently not a sin in Southern Baptist churches, because there were always plenty of smokers gathered outside of church doors before and after services. Drinking, on the other hand, had to be conducted stealthily. Liquor store drive-thrus were very popular in the Bible Belt. I remember getting excited when going through the drive-thru with my dad, because the tellers always passed out suckers to kids who were along for the ride.

For some reason, we eventually stopped going to church for a period of time. When we took it up again, we began attending the Liberty 86 Community Church near Bug Scuffle Community. Eighty-six, as we called it, was about half an hour's drive away from our house, but in the opposite direction of Little Elm – so in the direction opposite of civilization. Eighty-six was an old one-room schoolhouse in school district 86 that now serves as an old one-room church. Granny's son L.V. was (and still is) the pastor. At the time that we attended, the entire congregation was made up of five families: the Vickerys (L.V.'s family), the Kuharicks (my family), the Sherrys, the Cokers and the Bresslers.

The specials at 86 were usually spontaneous as opposed to prepared in advance, but they were just as exciting. The trio of LeAnn and Susan Vickery and Jodi Sherry were crowd favorites, especially when they sang "I'll Fly Away," Really, any Albert E. Brumley song was a favorite ("Turn Your Radio On," "Victory in Jesus," "He Set Me Free," etc.). I also enjoyed hearing Mr. Bressler play his harmonica. Milton Vickery, one of Granny's grandsons, would visit on occasion and could always be coerced to sing a stunning rendition of "Oh What a Savior."

The baptism of an 86 member was an absolutely joyous occasion. Members of the congregation would take a field trip several miles down the dirt road to a clearing along Fall Creek. I was baptized at Little Elm in a baptistery, which is basically a big bathtub that was permanently built in to the back of the stage. This was definitely a spiritually powerful event in my life, but it still does not compare to the energy and symbolism of a baptism outdoors in the middle of a running creek. L.V. baptized George and Mary Jane in Fall Creek. George's was the first creek baptism that I'd witnessed. As his head was dunked under water, I could tangibly sense that all of his sins to that point flowed out of his body and into the creek and then were simply "washed away," just like the way we would sing about from the old hymnals.

On Sunday evenings, there was time set aside for testimonials. Usually people would go up on stage to recount stories of how God had answered their prayers and met their needs. One evening my dad showed up completely drunk and decided to do something different with his testimonial time. He decided he was going to preach. Dad only got a few nonsensical words out before he fell hard to his knees as if he'd been shoved from behind. He looked all around the room as he slowly stood up and then spun around to see who was behind him. No one. He brushed himself off and commenced with his sermon. Blam! His knees hit the stage again. This time Dad decided to wrap up the sermon and sat back down in the pew. After the service Doris Coker approached Dad and said, "I believe you felt the power of the

Lord." Dad, still a little drunk and dazed, told her, "Yeah. He just knocked the *$#% out of me!"

Granny's Inferno

I read Dante's Inferno for the first time in my Freshman English class in college. I was (and still am) absolutely intrigued by the author's choices of punishments to coincide with different types of sins.

There were three types of punishments at Granny's house. These involved a fly swatter, a bed and a toilet - the latter was by far the most dreaded. In Dante's Inferno, the punishments fit the crimes. In Granny's Inferno, the punishments were doled out randomly according to how many kids were implicated, but they were equally interesting choices.

One form of punishment was a good old-fashioned whupping with the fly swatter. This was announced by Granny very matter-of-factly: "I am going to whup you with the fly swatter." Then she would proclaim to another child: "Go and git me the fly swatter." This task was always carried out enthusiastically. Getting whupped with the fly swatter never hurt. Granny took it very seriously and she was plenty mad when she wielded it, but we all thought it was funny.

Corey's middle name is Sean. Granny refused to pronounce Sean as Shawn because that was completely ridiculous – everyone knows that Sean is pronounced Seen. I remember one afternoon when Corey got into some mischief that warranted the fly swatter. Granny chased him around the front yard with the red fly swatter yelling: "Corey Seen, you get back here! I am going to whup you with the fly swatter". When the whupping finally commenced, she broke her fly swatter on Corey Seen's butt. I bet she never Seen that coming. We all laughed so hard, Corey hardest of all.

Another form of punishment was to be sent under Granny's bed. It was a small twin bed covered with a tan bedspread that had short tassels along the edges that hung down nearly to the floor. The accused had to lie down and butt-scoot underneath the bed. Then Granny would start talking smack: "I just seen a huge spider under there yesterday evening." We didn't believe her, but it was sooooo boring. At least the fly swatter was quick. I twisted those tassels. I braided those tassels. I tied those tassels. Those tassels were the only thing going. Now I wonder why we never thought preemptively to roll a toy car or a ball or something under there.

The final and most dreaded form of punishment at Granny's house was to sit on the pot, a.k.a. the toilet. (Don't let the presence of a pot fool you - Granny didn't have indoor plumbing either.) This punishment was usually reserved for times when more than one child was at fault. "You go git under the bed and *you* go sit on the pot!" It was a loathsome experience. The only saving grace was that the pot was near the bed, so it was sometimes possible to whisper back and forth.

I remember one time when I was happily reminiscing with a friend about being whupped with a fly swatter and forced under a bed and onto a toilet as punishment. I was caught off-guard by the shocked reaction: "Well, that's child abuse!" Huh, I never thought of it that way before. And I still don't. Kids know when they're loved.

Hillbilly Justice on the School Bus

As I already mentioned, we lived on top of a remote dirt road mountain. The roads were not maintained properly; almost not at all. It is not clear if the poor roads kept it off of the school bus route or if the roads were poorly maintained because they were not on a school bus route. Regardless of the reasoning, my parents had to drive us about 15 minutes down the mountain and across the blacktop to the neighboring dirt road mountain to catch the bus.

Most busses were based at the school, but my bus was based in Granny's driveway. Olan, Granny's son, drove my school bus. My parents dropped us off at Granny's house early in the morning and we would get on the bus when Olan came down from his house to start it. Our bus route wound up Granny's dirt road mountain and around on top of it and back down it. The route was at least an hour long one way. We were first on the bus in the mornings and last off the bus in the afternoons. I spent a lot of time on the bus.

Olan was a cool bus driver. He once took up an offering from the kids and purchased an 8-track cassette player. He mounted the player above his head by the driver's seat and ran some wires and speakers to the back of the bus. It was glorious! Ours was the only bus with music, which was a big deal since this was before portable music from iPods and iPhones, and only a few wealthy kids had Walkmans and Boomboxes. I still associate a very limited subset of music to this time, namely Electric Avenue by Eddy Grant and pretty much every Eagles song ever available on 8-track at the time.

Our school bus picked up kids from kindergarten through 12th grade, so there were plenty of characters of various ages. Olan had his mother's knack for keeping order. The youngest kids sat in the front and the oldest in the back. I really don't remember too many noteworthy incidences. Except one.

In addition to babysitting the four of us, Granny also sat for many other children off and on, including the two Joshes, Josh Pride and Little Josh. Despite their names, they were both around the same age and build. One particular day, the two Joshes started arguing and broke into a fist fight. Olan was yelling at them from the driver's seat to stop, but they continued. Well, Olan got fed up and brought the bus to a stop. He told the two Joshes to come to the front of the bus and face one another. He told Josh Pride to hit Little Josh just as hard as he could. Josh Pride grinned from ear to ear and did it. Little Josh started hollering and sobbing while Josh Pride continued to grin. Next, Olan told Little Josh to hit Josh Pride as hard as he could. You can bet Little Josh was happy to oblige, and he belted Josh Pride a good one. Both boys stood there hunched over and crying and in pain in the front of the bus while we all stared at them. Olan instructed the two Joshes to go and sit down, and they did. I'm still not completely sure what the lesson was, but I'm convinced that there was one.

Olan and Granny and all of the Vickerys were very likable. Even so, some of them were a little prone to mischief, including Uncle Rue. Rue was actually his middle name. His first name was, perhaps fittingly, Wiley. Josh Pride and his parents, Beth and Luther, eventually moved off of our mountain, and Luther arranged for Uncle Rue to rent their trailer. So Uncle Rue moved from Granny's mountain to our mountain. This didn't last long. Uncle Rue ended up selling Luther's trailer to someone he met at the Shamrock bar near Lincoln. He even went so far as to help the guy move Luther's trailer off of the mountain. Uncle Rue took the money and fled to Texas for a brief time until things settled down and then moved back in with Granny.

Yard Apes out Yonder

Granny's house was our second home, and Granny was…well, our Granny. We ate many meals of brown beans and cornbread at Granny's house. Orange Kool-Aid was also a staple. It had to be orange because Granny said that all of the other colors caused cancer. The best part of the Kool-Aid was at the bottom where all of the white sugar rested. There was a 55-gallon metal drum near the right side of her house that she called the rain barrel. I saw mosquito larvae on top many times when I peered into the rain barrel. I secretly knew that this was the water that was used to make the Kool-Aid, but I drank it anyway. What are you going to do?

Granny read faithfully from her King James Bible every day. It is the only book that I ever saw her read. Granny lived out life with honesty and integrity, and her word was binding. As much as she believed the ancient written Word of God, she did not believe in the scientific discoveries of modern times. Granny tried to set us straight whenever the topics presented themselves. The Earth was only a few thousand years old - not millions of years, because God created the Earth in seven days, and the year was only 1980 whatever. There were no such things as dinosaurs because there was no mention of them in the Bible. The Earth was not round, but flat. You can look as far as the eye can see, and you will never see a curvature. And, of course, men have never gone to the moon. She used to site as evidence some unknown news broadcast in which three men went up in the rocket and four came down.

Granny was full of interesting idioms, such as "I'll be swan on to goodness!' and my personal favorite, "You could stink a dead dog off a gut wagon." When we got rowdy and restless, she used to lament, "You kids are behaving like a bunch of wild yard apes - now git out yonder and play!" Yonder was anywhere outside, except for sometimes when yonder would be transformed into a very specific yet elusive location: "No, I said out *yonder*" (with the point of a finger). Even though we weren't supervised most of the time when we were outside, we never strayed from Granny's yard. The unspoken boundaries were the driveway and the white pom-pom bush in the far corner of the front yard and the clothes line and the outhouse in the back yard. We weren't allowed out in the old smoke house, but every once in a great while we would get brave and sneak inside. The smoke house was a forbidden wonderland filled with all sorts of stored items, most of them happily dangerous to small children.

Corey, Josh, George and I played endless hours outside. Henry eventually joined in as he got older. Sometimes we would climb the tree in Granny's front yard. Sometimes we would play a game of makeshift baseball in the back yard using a stick for a bat and a rock for a ball. Sometimes we would play "roll the barrel" in which we would lay an empty 55-gallon drum on its side and then see who could run on it the furthest without falling off (yet another use for those versatile barrels - I can't believe I don't currently own one!). We even had our own club called the Pee Wad Hockey Wad Squad, perhaps to celebrate my newly learned word. BTW, hockey is #2, as in "I have to go hockey". I have no idea why we called it that. We even made up a little song about the Pee Wad Hockey Wad Squad. To this day, I'm still a fan of bathroom humor.

The only animals that Granny had were chickens in a small coop near the outhouse. Granny gathered their eggs and wrung their necks for food. Granny would take a chicken by the neck and somehow snap and spin it so that the head separated from the body. We would chase the headless chickens as they ran around the yard. Headless chickens can run surprisingly fast and have quite a bit of stamina, and they are impossible to catch because they switch up direction often and without warning. After a few minutes, the bodies would just sort of stop and fall over. Sometimes when Granny was mad at us, she would say, "You kids! I'd like to wring your little necks." We would usually perk up and pay attention to that.

Granny would bring the dead chicken into the kitchen and pluck the feathers out and then chop it up for cooking. As part of the preparation, she would remove developing eggs from the dead chicken's body, claiming that these were good, edible eggs. She would cook these up and then present them in a bowl on the dinner table along with the cooked chicken meat. I ate them. She was right.

Salt and Salve
a.k.a. Henry Gets Potty Trained

Granny was very knowledgeable in the art of hillbilly home remedies. Sometimes she would rub lin'ment on her sore calves in the evenings. This was interesting because it was a process that I never saw at home and because it was the only time we ever saw Granny's calves. The scent was a very poignant mix of mint and medicine. Open wounds called for rubbin' alcohol followed by fresh aloe vera from a piece that was broken from Granny's large potted plant in the living room.

Chronic coughing required a spoonful of salt. If you don't think this sounds too bad, then you've never eaten a spoonful of salt all at once by itself. I remember holding my breath and concentrating really hard on something in the distance in the hopes of staving the urge to cough. Passing out would have also been warmly welcomed – anything to avoid having to eat that spoonful of salt. If one spoonful didn't do the trick, another would be administered. Maybe it really worked. I don't remember eating more than two spoonfuls. Maybe I passed out.

I was five and George was four when we started going to Granny's house, but Henry was just a baby. There came a time when Henry was three years old that Granny grew impatient with my parents' failed efforts to potty train Henry and decided to kindly assist in this endeavor.

Granny had an old wringer washer, the kind with an upright barrel. The washing machine was in the bathroom, which is rather fitting for this story. It was actually a laundry room/bathroom/food pantry, but the food pantry part is irrelevant for this story. Granny filled the barrel of the washing machine and then gave Henry fair warning that the next time he peed in his pants, she was going to immerse him in scalding hot water.

It wasn't long before Henry did indeed pee his pants. Granny ran over and scooped him up, and we ran over to see if Granny was really going to go through with it. Henry was petrified as Granny took him into the bathroom, held him over the barrel, announced again that it was filled with scalding hot water, and then dunked him in. Henry screamed bloody murder, "It's hot! I'm burning!" We stood there staring in shock. Then Granny started rocking back and forth, cackling like a hen. She pulled Henry out of the water and dried him off. She took on an instructional tone and calmly explained to us that the water was actually freezing cold but that the stinging sensation of the cold water combined with the image that she'd embedded in Henry's mind just made him *think* that the water was really scalding hot. Henry was potty trained from that day forward and also scarred for life.

Poor Henry, bless his heart, was also an avid thumb-sucker. Well, it just so happened that Granny had a remedy for that, too. She would dip his thumb in turpentine while he was napping. I think I also speak for my brother George when I say "Praise God!" that I was already potty trained and did not suck my thumb when I met Granny.

If the Hills Could Speak

The way my family lived was not the exception but the rule in Cove Creek Community. Most of us lived on dirt roads, drove beater cars, and had no running water. In fact, the Prairie Grove city water lines did not even run out to Cove Creek until 1995 – three years after I graduated from high school. Even then, this amenity was optional and many families declined the opportunity because each family had to pay for the pipes and installation from the main road to their houses. Anyway, we were all in the same boat, and relationships among the hill people were generally good. We had to take the good with the bad in people and learned to be very tolerant and forgiving of one another.

Truth be told, there are still many families even today in Cove Creek and Hogeye and Bug Scuffle and the surrounding communities who live exactly as I describe my childhood that was now three decades ago. In many ways, this life is every American's stereotypical image of the life of an Arkansas hillbilly: barefoot, dirty, technologically impaired and physically demanding. But hill people *ain't* stupid and they *is* resourceful and persevering. They are kind-hearted with a touch of wiliness and a whole lot of spunk.

In 1953 Mrs. Emerson was valedictorian of her graduating class of 11 at Poughkeepsie High School in Sharp County, Arkansas. When she was 49 years old, Mrs. Emerson decided that she wanted to go to college. She fought for and was eventually granted a scholarship from the University of Arkansas based on her valedictorian status from 30 years prior, and she graduated with her teaching degree in 1988. After 13 years of teaching, Mrs. Emerson retired and has since written two books under the name of Geneva King Emerson and also contributes folk stories to such magazines as the Ozark Mountaineer.

My mother began nursing school when Mary Jane was a baby. She graduated with honors from the University of Arkansas' R.N. program in 1983, even though she worked, had four kids, and lived on the mountain in Cove Creek Community. She has been a practicing nurse ever since, in addition to being a lactation consultant and a Lamaze instructor. Dad is the unassuming genius who reads encyclopedias and takes AutoCAD classes for fun. George has a Master's degree and Henry and Mary Jane have also gone to college.

I myself am not unusually smart, but I *am* exceptionally perseverant. I am who I am because of my parents and my Granny and all of the Vickerys and the Emersons and the fly swatter whuppings and the brown cars and the salt eating and the chicken neck wringing. I hope that I have served well as a voice for the hills. Praise God!

Hillbilly Photos

Normal Neighborhood in Cleveland

Mom holding me in our neighborhood on East 33rd Street in Cleveland.

Normal House in Cleveland

Dad blowing bubbles in our living room on East 33rd Street in Cleveland with me and my dog Bonzo.

International Harvester Travelall

George and I playing in the dirt next to the International Harvester Travelall a.k.a. the Green Truck that we drove to Arkansas when we moved from Ohio.

Army Tent

Dad with Bonzo getting ready to pitch our new home on Hoot Owl Mountain.

Building the Cabin 1

Dad cutting the wood paneling for the cabin walls.

Building the Cabin 2

Almost done.

Lanterns and Porch

Sitting on the front porch of the cabin. A Coleman lantern hangs on the side of the cabin and another one sits on the ground to the left of the porch.

Kids in Front of Cabin

Henry, George and I on the porch of the cabin pretending we're Indians. My wonderful white goat Summer is on the right in the background.

Propane Stove and Fridge

George in the cabin beside the propane stove and refrigerator. The wood stove is on the right.

George in Cabin

George in the cabin beside the wood stove near the stairs leading to the loft.

Cabin Christmas

Christmas in the cabin, 1979. George, Henry and I with our handmade paper ornaments hung on our Charlie Brown tree. We would always receive boxes of gifts from our grandparents and other relatives in Ohio. To the right is our huge porcelain sink.

Artificial Turf Carpet

Henry sitting on the floor of the cabin with its green artificial turf carpet.

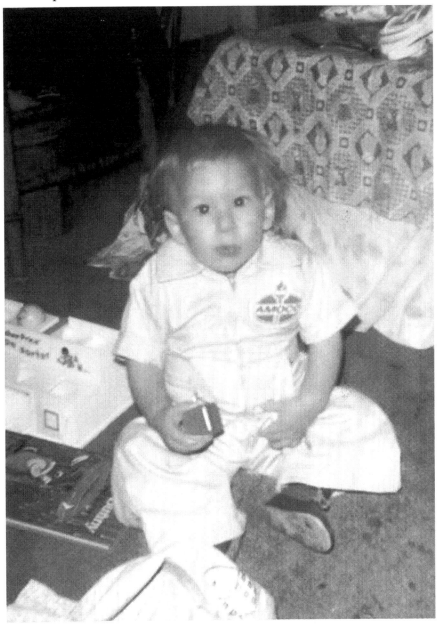

Snack Time

George and I chillaxing eating a snack with our toys and a stray cat.

Bathtub

Me taking a bath in pond water in the kiddie pool with a stray kitten.

Tractor and Beetle

Mom driving the tractor with our Volkswagen Beetle (pre-fire days) in the background.

Laundry

Laundry on the clothesline stretching from the trailer to the pond.

Mom on Porch

Mom standing on the porch connecting the cabin and the trailer.

George in Trailer with Guns

George in the living room of the trailer standing beside the wood stove with our gun rack on the back wall.

Dad with Fish

Dad standing between our pond and the trailer with a fish he caught in the pond.

Fishing in Cowboy Boots

Dad fishing in shorts and cowboy boots at the Blue Hole.

Blue Hole 1

Dad getting ready to jump off of the bluff at the Blue Hole. The low part of the bluff on the left is where we would hoist ourselves out of the water after swimming across.

Blue Hole 2

George and I swimming in the Blue Hole. We are in the foreground looking at the camera. The others are strangers who also showed up to swim, one in a dress.

Dresser Drawer Crib

Henry, George and I with Mary Jane in the dresser drawer. This worked so well in the cabin with Henry that it was also used in the trailer with Mary Jane.

Dancing in Trailer

Hillbilly dancing in the trailer, probably to "Love Me Do" by the Beatles.

Driveway

The good part of the driveway. The driveway got bad where it took a sharp left curve downward where the truck is parked.

Granny with Hammer and Barrel

Granny standing next to Mom coming out her front door. On the bottom left is the rusty 55-gallon steel drum with her hammer sitting on top.

Granny in Kitchen 1

Granny in her kitchen wearing one of her typical short-sleeved dresses.

Granny in Kitchen 2

Granny holding Mary Jane in her kitchen. See the way she looks at Mary Jane, the Chosen One.

The Two Joshes

The two Joshes, Little Josh on the left and Josh Pride on the right, sitting on the steps leading to the trail from Granny's house to Olan's house.

Devil's Den

Our family standing beneath one of the wet weather waterfalls on the Devil's Den Self-Guided Trail at Devil's Den State Park in West Fork.

Flower Bed and Tire Swing

Mary Jane standing in Mom's flower garden in front of the cabin and trailer with our tire swing in the background.

Henry by the Wood Pile

Henry looking darn cute out by the wood pile.

George on Canon

George blowing a bubble sitting on the canon of one of the M40 self-propelled artillery vehicles at the Battlefield Park in Prairie Grove.

Castle

George in the tower of "Seven Points", a.k.a. "The Castle" at Wilson Park in Fayetteville.

Scout

International Harvester Scout parked in front of my grandparents'
house on East 66th Street in Cleveland.

Plymouth Fury

On the left is the winner of the Ugliest Car Award, the Plymouth Fury in all of its brown glory with its peeling vinyl top. Henry, George, Mary Jane and I are sitting on a Pontiac Grand Prix, another ugly brown car. Another old non-running car is in the background.

Liberty 86 Church

The men hanging out on the steps of the Liberty 86 Community Church near Bug Scuffle. Pastor L.V., Granny's son, is sitting second from the left. Milton, Granny's grandson, is sitting on the top step furthest to the right. Dad is standing.

Fall Creek Baptism

Pastor L.V. baptizing George in Fall Creek.

Family Picture

Family picture taken in front of our pond. Note the cigarette in Dad's left hand. A similar picture from this photo shoot went out on a Christmas card, cigarette and all.

Made in the USA
San Bernardino, CA
13 July 2016